Acknowlegements

MW00949312

I would like to thank the Adam's County historical society in Brighton, Colorado for opening their doors and allowing us to film, along with the very talented actors and actresses of Big Fish talent in Denver, Colorado. Also a special thanks to Leonard Garduno Photography for his expertise and sharp eye, and to Gretchen Ricker for helping me put this awesome project together.

Who is J. F. Nichols?

For years, I had an old yellowed piece of paper, tattered at the edges that carried a poem about a sickly little boy longing for love and acceptance. It had been passed down to me by my mother who heard it at her high school graduation and fell in love with it. At the bottom of the right hand corner was one word. "Anonymous." I often wondered who this author was, but early research revealed nothing. Then one day I came across an 1887 graduation brochure found on the internet. The two day commencement ceremony listed a full Schedule of poetry reading and classical music. One of the poems during this time was "Tommy's Prayer," By J. F. Nichols. Finally I found you....that is to say, I found your name. More research led me to a John F. Nichols who lived from about 1800-1850, but is this the same J. F. who wrote the amazing poem? That is still the question. Regardless of who you were Mr. Nichols, your poem has passed the test of time and lives in the hearts of many generations.

I pray my interpretation of your story pleases you and all who have found comfort from a crippled little boy and a Savior who loved him so much he sent a messenger to show him the way home.

M. K. Boyle

In a dark and dismal alley

where the sunshine never came...

Dwelt a little lad named Tommy.
Sickly...
        Delicate...
                and Lame.

He was six,
was little Tommy
twas just five years ago...

When his

drunken

mother

dropped

him...

He had never known the comfort
of a mothers tender care

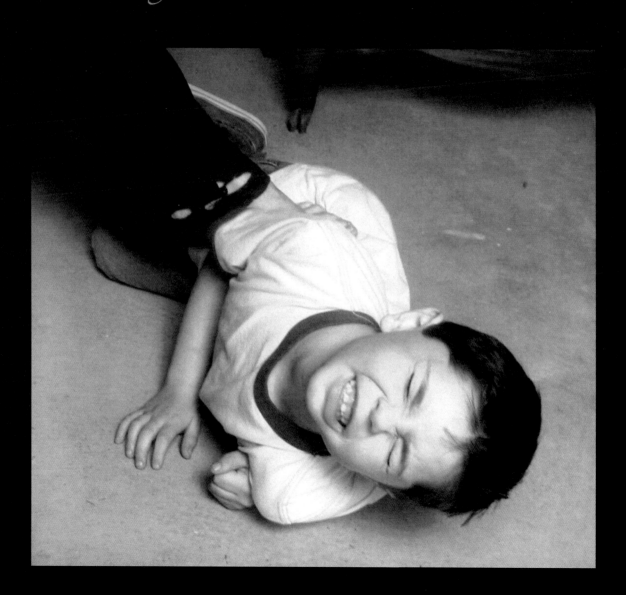

made his pain yet worse to bare

There he lay in the cellar from the morning
'till the night...

Starved, neglected, ill-treated,
cursed not to make his dull life bright

For he know not of the Savior
or the Heaven up above

Floating up the alley, walking inward from the street, came a voice of someone singing, singing so clear... so sweet.

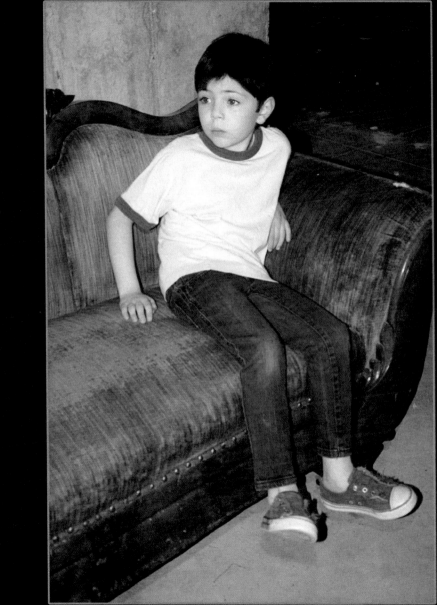

Eagerly did Tommy listen
as the singing nearer came.

Oh that he could see
the singer.

How he wished
he weren't lame.

Then he called and shouted loudly 'till
the singer heard the sound,
and noting where it issued the little cripple found.

Twas a maiden
rough and ragged,
hair unkept and
naked feet.

All her garments
torn and ratted,
her appearance...
far from neat.

"So yer called me," said the maiden,
 "Wonder what yer wants of me?

"Most folks call me Singing Jesse
What may yer name chance to be?"

"My names Tommy
I'm a cripple and I
loves to here you sing,
for it makes me feel
so happy.

Sing me something,
anything!"

Jesse laughed and answered smiling

"I can't stay so very long, but I'll sing a hymn to please ya, what I calls the 'Glory song.'"

Then she sang to him of Heaven,

Pearly Gates and Streets of Gold...

Where the happy angel children are not

But where happiness and gladness

never can decrease or end,

Where the kind and loveing Jesus

Oh how Tommy's eyes did glisten, as he drank in every word.

As it came from Singing Jesse

Is it true this he had heard?

Then he said to Singing Jesse,

"Is there really such a place?"

and a tear began to trickle down his palid little face

"Tommy, yer a heathen why it's up beyond the sky

So the little ragged singing girl who had
learned in Sunday school...

Taught little cripple
Tommy how to love
and how to pray.

kissed his cheek and went away

Tommy lay within the cellar which had grown so dark and cold...

Thinking about all the children in the shiny streets of Gold.

He heeded not the dampness
of the dark and chilly room,

for the joy of Tommy's bosom
could disperse the deepest gloom.

"Oh if I can only see it!"
Thought the cripple as he lay.

So I thinks I'll try and pray."

So he put his hands
together, and he
closed his little eyes,

In an accent weak,
yet earnest, sent his
message to the sky.

Gentle Jesus,
please forgive,
as I didn't
know afore,

That you care
for little cripples
that are weak
and very poor."

Jesse came ter day,

and told me all about you, so I wants to

try and pray.

You can see me, can't you Jesus
Jesse told me you could.
And somehow I must believe it for it
seems so prime and good,

And she told
me if I loved
you, I can see
you when I die.

In a bright happy Heaven
that is up beyond the sky.

Lord, I'm just a
cripple, and I'm
no use here below.

For I've heard my mother say

she'd be glad if I could go.

And I'm cold and hungry... sometimes.

And I feel so lonely too.

*Can't you take me
with you Gentle
Jesus,
up to Heaven
along with you?*

Oh I'd be so good and gentle and I
would never cry or fret, and your kindness
to me Jesus I would surely nay forget.

I would love you all I know of
and never make a noise,

Can't you find me just a corner
where I can watch the other boys?

Oh I think you'll
do it Jesus,

Something sort of
tells me so.

For I feel so glad
and happy and
I do want to go.

How I long

to see you

Jesus

and the

children a

so bright

Come and fetch me, won't you Jesus?

Tommy ceased
his supplication
he had told his
soul's desire,

and he waited
for his answer
until his head
began to tire.

Then he turned toward a corner and laid in a huddled heap,

Closed his eyes so gently and quickly fell asleep.

He had only heard of Jesus from a ragged singing girl.

He might have
wondered pondered
till his mind began
to whirl.

But he took it
as she said it.

He believed it
then and there...

Simply trusting in the Savior,

Tommy's prayer had soon been answered

and happy home.

Cast

Tommy.............................. Jackson Diego

Jesse.............................. Jami Boyle

Jesus.............................. Todd Leopold

                                   Ryan Anderson

Mother............................ Brooklyne Coulter

Teacher........................... AnneMarie Anderson

Angels............................ Grant Anderson

                                   Virginia Anderson

                                   Benjamin Braiman

                                   Lauren Boyle

                                   Caige Coulter

                                   Sam Delossantos

                                   Maliah Howard

                                   Maya Howard

                                   Damir Schebler

                                   Alexander Lindahl

                                   Ethan Lindahl

                                   Micah Lindahl

School Children................... Tia Amaral-Elkins

                                   Sam Delossantos

                                   Spencer Lintonsmith

                                   Sierra Orteza-Santopietro

                                   Abby Williams

Baby Tommy........................ Zane Cokewell

About the Author

M.K. Boyle lives outside of Denver, Colorado.

She has written 2 books Consisting of 52 sketches
for church and youth groups entitled, "Acting
up in Church I and II"

She is an author, Nurse, Public speaker and business
entrepreneur.

She is a member of the Christian's Writers Guild